WITCH-HUNT

the Great Essex Witch Scare of 1582

Anthony Harris

IAN HENRY PUBLICATIONS

ISBN 0 86025 518 2

The illustration on the cover
is taken from
Prodigorum ac Ostentorum Chronicon
[The Chronicle of Prodigies
and Curiosities]
by Conrad Lycosthenus
printed in Basel in 1577

Published by
Ian Henry Publications, Ltd.
20 Park Drive, Romford, Essex RM1 4LH
and printed by
ColourBooks Ltd.,
Baldoyle, Dublin, Ireland

CHAPTER ONE

Wednesday, February the nineteenth, 1582

St Clere's Hall, St Osyth, in the county of Essex

The presiding magistrate: Brian Darcy, Lord of the Manor, Justice of the Peace

The great mediæval central hall, with its soaring hammer-beam roof, falls silent at the entry of Brian Darcy, Lord of the Manor, Justice of the Peace. The onlookers - petty officials, witnesses, sensation seekers - who are crammed into every corner of the double-aisled hall, watch as the accused woman, flanked by two village constables, rises to face him. Her name is Ursula Kemp. The charge is murder - murder by witchcraft.

●●●●●

Over recent weeks and months the town of St Osyth and the surrounding area had been beset by an ever-growing series of mishaps and catastrophes, too many to be explained away as mere accidents or tragic coincidences. A pair of horses had dropped dead at the plough; pigs 'skipped and leaped' about their yard before they too died; calves had miscarried, cows produced milk contaminated with blood, others had died in their pasture, followed within days by the deaths of the farmer himself and his wife. A three month old child fell from its cradle and broke its neck, whilst its mother developed a 'lameness in her bones, especially in her legs', an ailment which was also afflicting many of her neighbours. Two other children had been struck down with mysterious illnesses and, although one recovered, its mother too had died.

The Great Hall of St Clere's Hall

And John Johnson, the Collector for the Poor, and his wife had both fallen ill and died.

The thousand inhabitants of St Osyth would have been more than ready to agree that in the midst of life they were in death. Their average life expectancy was no more than thirty-two years, although this figure does to some extent give a distorted view because of the infant mortality rate, with one in four children not surviving beyond its first year - and no doubt many more deaths, especially of still-born or illegitimate offspring, went unrecorded - and a death rate of 18% for one to five year olds.

Even so, in this enclosed, claustrophobic community - little more than a village - hemmed in by dank mudflats and creeks, and the bleak marshlands stretching away to the mouths of the Rivers Colne and Blackwater, where petty grievances could fester and malicious gossip become unquestioned fact, these and many other misfortunes of everyday life had taken on a sinister significance.

All the victims of these calamities were known to have fallen foul of women already suspected of being witches. The cradle-death mother had told one that she had asked someone else to act as nurse for her new-born child. In his rôle as Collector, Johnson dispensed charity to the needy in the form of money or food, but he had turned down an old woman's plea for twelve pence to succour her sick husband and she had been heard loudly berating him for his meanness. The neighbour of another woman, listening through their flimsy partition wall, overheard her cursing the Collector for giving her bread too hard-baked to eat. The farmer's wife had fallen out with her neighbour, beating her pigs and stabbing one with a pitchfork after they had strayed on their land.

Within days - or in some cases hours - of all these disputes, disaster had struck. Over twenty people had died and the truth was inescapable. Satanic forces were at work in St Osyth. There was in their midst a vipers' nest of witchcraft that had to be rooted out.

Perhaps because of its relatively isolated situation, Essex does seem to have been particularly prone to such scares. Between 1560 and 1680 more witchcraft cases were heard at the County's Assizes than in the combined courts of Surrey, Hertfordshire, Kent, and Sussex, all fellow-members of the Home Circuit. they reached a peak in the 1580s when they formed 13% of all criminal cases, and it was of course at the Chelmsford Assizes of 1645 that the twenty-eight women rounded up by Matthew Hopkins, the self-styled Witchfinder-General, were tried.

In normal circumstances, people who believed themselves bewitched would first try to help themselves. When, for example, their ale refused to brew or butter to set, the traditional remedy was to plunge into it a piece of red-hot iron - preferably a horseshoe. In the case of illness, they could consult a local wiseman or woman who, with a blend of herbal concoctions and spells, could use 'white' magic to drive out the evil forces that afflicted them.

Several of those waiting to give evidence had tried such remedies but these had all failed and they were now looking to a higher power to protect them. They had not though turned to the church. The only priest to figure in the St Osyth story is Richard Harrison, pastor of the nearby parish of Little Oakley, whose own wife took to her bed and died, convinced that she was bewitched. 'What will the people say,' he begged, 'that I being a preacher should have my wife so weak in faith?' But none of his prayers and exhortations could save her.

Even though the church in post-Reformation England followed the Roman Catholic teaching that witchcraft was a mortal sin, deriving its power from a pact with the devil, it displayed a generally relaxed attitude towards those who were suspected of practising the black arts. The ecclesiastical courts could investigate such cases - one of the women due to appear before Darcy had also received a summons from her local spiritual court - but in the main it was content to leave these matters to the civil authorities.

So the St Osyth folk turned to Brian Darcy for salvation - and he would not let them down. Under his skilful manipulation, in an atmosphere of rising terror and hysteria, confessions would be extracted, ever more fantastic allegations made. Friend would accuse friend, sister denounce sister, child betray mother, so that within a week five women from the town would be consigned to Colchester Gaol to await trial for their lives. And he would not stop there. Within a month his net would spread to the neighbouring villages of Little Clacton, Little Oakley, Thorpe-le-Soken, and Walton to enmesh a further eight suspects, making thirteen in all - twelve women and one man, the classic formula for a witches' coven.

St Clere's Hall

Although Darcy could not fail to be aware of this, the evidence that he would amass creates a picture far removed from the romanticised image of broomstick-riding maidens flying off to naked churchyard orgies. Reginald Scot's *The Discoverie of Witchcraft*, which was published just two years after these events and was in fact directly inspired by them, gives us a vivid picture of the typical witch of this time.

●●●●●

One sort of such as are said to be witches are women which be commonly old, lame, blear-eyed, foul and fill of wrinkles. They are lean and deformed, showing melancholy in their faces, to the horror of all that see them. These miserable creatures are so odious to their neighbours, and so feared, as few dare offend them, or deny them anything they ask; whereby they take upon them - yea, and sometimes think - that they can do such things as are beyond the ability of human nature.

●●●●●

Darcy had his own private reasons for convening this trial for he saw in it the chance to realize a long-cherished dream. He was a member of a cadet line of the family, based in Tolleshunt D'Arcie, and all his life he had been in the shadow of his two older brothers, sons of their father Thomas's first marriage, whilst his mother, Elizabeth, was herself a widow before her remarriage. Moreover, with his manor house of St Clere's lying within half a mile of St Osyth, with the formidable profile of its Priory clearly visible across the marshes, he must constantly have been aware of his illustrious kinsmen, the

Barons Darcy of Chiche - the title deriving from the Anglo-Saxon settlement from which St Osyth had developed. Over the last thirty years they had transformed the twelfth century Priory into a magnificent private residence, where Queen Elizabeth herself had twice been entertained. The second Baron, another Thomas, had died just over a year before - his death too had been the subject of dark whisperings - and had been succeeded by his sixteen year old son. So now Brian Darcy saw the chance to establish a reputation in his own right, and in a cause that he eagerly embraced.

For many years he had harboured an obsessive hatred of 'the devilish and damnable practice' of witchcraft. For him, hanging was too merciful a fate for 'sorcerers, witches and the rest of that hellish livery' and he looked with chagrin across the Channel to continental Europe, where witchcraft was seen as a heresy to be ruthlessly stamped out. Offenders were brought before the Inquisition and other ecclesiastical courts and when found guilty - as happened almost invariably - they were burned at the stake.

The English courts, on the other hand, could only impose the death penalty if it had been proved that witchcraft had been employed to commit murder or the treasonable device of prophesying how long the Queen would reign and who would succeed her. All other offence were punished by a session in the pillory and the maximum of a year's imprisonment. So it was that, whilst in Europe between the fourteenth and seventeenth centuries, many thousands if not millions of so-called witches were tortured and burned, in England there were at most fuve hundred such executions - a figure exceeded in a single year, 1542, in the Italian city of Como alone - and these by the marginally more humane method of hanging.

This relative tolerance is reflected in the Essex court records from the mid-1500s to the late seventeenth century. Many so-called witches were freed before they even came to trial, and of the cases that were heard over 50% resulted in acquittals. Darcy had already come up against this enlightened attitude. Two years before he had suffered the humiliation of being ordered to release a thirteen year old boy, Thomas Lever, whom he was holding without trial on suspicion of being a magician's accomplice, after the boy's mother had petitioned the Privy Council in London. As Justice of the Peace, he had wide-ranging powers and could impose the death penalty for a variety of offenses, but the allegations on this present case were so serious that the accused would have to go on to face trial at the Chelmsford Assize. He would have to ensure, therefore, that such a strong case was built up that there would be no escaping the gallows.

To begin with, he had chosen to hold the hearings on home territory. Although his main residence was Tiptree Manor, he also owned St Clere's Hall, which was - and still is - after the Priory, by far the most imposing residence in St Osyth. It stands half a mile outside the town, on the very edge of the marshes, surrounded by a moat which, as they crossed it, would have underlined for the accused just how cut off they were from the known and familiar of their own humble dwellings. The great hall would provide a suitably intimidating setting, whilst more intimate adjoining rooms together with his private garden were also on hand for the one to one sessions he also planned to employ.

He had made a close study of the accounts of continental witch trials, in particular Jean Bodin's *De la Demonamanie des Sorciers*, published just two years previously. In what was in effect his own personal courtroom, where he could act unchallenged as both judge and prosecuting counsel, he would put into practice the methods he so admired - methods that he knew full well were totally alien to the spirit and practice of English law. The presumption from the very outset of the prisoners' guilt, the readiness to accept hearsay and the flimsiest of evidence as indisputable proof, the blend of brutal threats and false promises of leniency in return for confessions and the betrayal of others, the use of young children to give damning evidence against their parents: all of these tactics, and many more, would play their part in this, his personal crusade against the powers of darkness.

●●●●●

The stage is set. The first witness had taken the stand. The trial has begun.

CHAPTER TWO

Until very recently, Grace Thurlow had had good reason to be grateful to Ursula Kemp. A year ago, when she was six months pregnant, her son Davey was struck down by illness so that he was 'strangely taken and greatly tormented.' A similar phrase was applied to the pigs that 'skipped and leaped' about the yard, so it is likely that the child was suffering from convulsions. Although not life-threatening, the symptoms - clenched teeth, rolling eyes, the body shaken by violent twitches and often a loss of consciousness - can be terrifying for a helpless onlooker, and all that Grace and her husband John could do to comfort him was move his bed to the chimney corner.

He was lying there one day when Ursula Kemp unexpectedly entered the room. 'She took him by the hand,' his mother told the court, 'saying, Ah, good child, how art thou laden, and so went thrice out of the doors. And every time when she came in she took the child by the hand and said Ah, good child, how art thou laden.'

Grace was well aware of Ursula Kemp's reputation as a healer. Everyone in the town knew that she had cured Page's wife and Gray's wife after both of them had been bewitched. So when, without another word, her visitor turned to go she stopped her, begging her to come again that night and help her son further. But another visit would not be necessary. 'I warrant thee, aye,' Ursula assured her, 'thy child shall do well enough.' And sure enough, for the first time for many weeks Davey fell into a peaceful sleep which lasted the entire night.

Next morning he was sufficiently recovered to be left and his mother seized the chance to take some of the grain they grew on their parcel of land to the town's thirteenth century tide-mill to be ground into flour. On the way she met Ursula, who asked her how the child was.

'He took good rest this night,' she replied. 'God be thanked.'

'Aye, aye,' came the confident response. 'I warrant thee, he shall do well.'

It seems clear that Ursula Kemp did indeed have some powers of healing. It began, as she tells Darcy later, some ten years previously when she herself was cured after travelling eight miles to consult 'one Cock's wife of Weeley, now deceased.' She was suffering from 'lameness in the bones', a widespread affliction in the St Osyth area.

Surrounded as it was by damp marshland, and with most of the houses having earth floors and just a covering of rushes, this was no doubt a symptom of arthritis or rheumatism. But to the sufferers it was seen as a sure sign that they had been bewitched,

She therefore sought help from a wisewoman, who taught her how to 'unwitch' herself by blending together pig's dung and chervil, holding them in her left hand, taking a knife in her right, pricking the mixture three times then throwing it into the fire. She then had to make three marks under a table with the knife before stabbing it into the wood. Three is the most powerful of magical numbers and it was also employed in the final stage of the ritual, when she was told to take three leaves of sage and three of St John's wort, boil them together in ale and drink it last thing at night and again in the morning.

If, as she claimed, her lameness was cured, this will have been thanks to the herbal concoction. Both sage and St John's wort were recommended for 'inward hurts' and 'all pains of the joints' by herbalists such as John Gerarde. In his *Herballe*, published in 1597, he advises that they should be steeped in wine but in the impoverished spheres in which most wisewomen operated ale was much more readily available, with most households brewing their own.

Until recent times, sage continued to be used to treat a variety of 'women's ailments' - menopausal problems, increasing the milk supply for nursing mothers and as a general uterine tonic - and today it is one of the hormone-containing herbs that provide an alternative to hormone replacement therapy. St John's wort or hypericum, with its bright yellow flowers that bloomed around the period of the summer solstice, was widely used in mediæval times as a weapon in the constant war against the powers of darkness. In Wales, sprigs were placed on the doors of hosues as a protection against evil spirits, and at St Cleer in Cornwall wreaths of the plant were hung around the holy well to drive out witches from the village. Today, it is one of the most widely used of medicinal herbs and is being increasingly employed by mainstream practitioners as an anti-depressant. Ursula Kemp, existing in a perennial state of poverty and ill-health, musy surely have suffered from the 'melancholy' that afflicted so many at that time, and the herb might well have helped to ease her mind, temporarily at least. She would have been far from alone in this state, and it is surely no coincidence that the witch-scare that erupted around her began late in February, certainly the dreariest time of the year

Having cured herself, Ursula went on to gain a reputation for healing others. Sometimes she was sent for, but on this occasion came to the child of her own accord - unless his mother was too wary of Darcy to admit that she had sought her help. In any case, she followed the customary pattern, with solemn ritual - again built around the magic three and performed, one feels, primarily to impress the watching Grace - preceding the actual healing process, although here, perhaps because of the nature of the illness, this is achieved not through a herbal concoction but by touch.

Many apparent cures of this sort have a psychosomatic basis but Davey Thurlow will have been too young for this to have played any part in his recovery - although if his mother was less stressed as a result of Ursula Kemp's intervention, this could well have transmitted itself to the child.

Healing by touch - the laying on of hands - has a history stretching far back in time and was practised in ancient cultures as divers as those of China, India, Egypt and Classical Greece. It is also, of course, found today, both in primitive societies and among practitioners of a variety of alternative and 'new age' therapies. Many of the latter believe that they can channel the healing power within themselves by attuning their own energy force with

Illustration from *Newes from Scotland*, showing the actions of Agnes Sampson and her coven, the North Berwick witches, raising a storm against King James VI's ship sailing from Denmark. Dr John Fian, as recorder of the coven, sits at the desk in the centre; witches drink wine in the cellar in the foreground

that of the patient. The source of this power - natural or spiritual - varies, but in the sixteenth century, when virtually all 'healers' were women, such activities were condemned as blasphemous attempts to re-enact Christ's miraculous driving out of devils - not to mention a challenge to the male-dominated medical world of the time.

Many of those who were persecuted as witches on the Continent were in fact no more than healers, and Gillis Duncan, one of a group of so-called witches from North Berwick who in 1591 were accused of plotting to kill King James VI (later James I of England) first aroused the suspicions of her master, David Seaton, when he discovered that she 'took in hand to help all such as were troubled or grieved with any kind of sickness or infirmity'.

Darcy then will have been delighted with Grace Thurlow's story, even if it did seem to cast his prisoner in a positive light. He would have heartily agreed with William Perkins who, in his 1608 *A Discourse of the Damned Art of Witchcraft* roundly declared that 'the most horrible and detestable monster is the good witch.'

Davey had accompanied his mother to the courtroom and when he was brought before him Darcy made sure that his clerk noted that 'the palms of the child's hands were turned where the backs should be and the backs in the place of the palms'. This distortion of the very hands which Ursula had held had either been with the boy from birth or was perhaps a result of the fits he had suffered. Either way though, this was further proof that occult forces were at work, for any physical deformity - whether it be Richard III's hump back or Anne Boleyn's sixth finger - was widely seen as being an outward sign of an individual's being under the influence of malign forces.

One of the main reasons for claiming that there was no such thing as a good witch was that many of those who started out as healers found it impossible not to use their supernatural reputations to gain revenge if they were crossed in any way. And Ursula Kemp was one of these. Even before her 'healing' of Davey Thurlow, dark rumours had been spreading about her. Throughout her trial and gaol records, she is consistently referred to as 'alias Grey' and among the insults hurled at her, inside and out of the courtroom, she is frequently called 'whore'. One wonders therefore if, despite - or even because of - her ministrations, Gray's wife had died and she had moved in with the grieving widower. Certainly; she had at least one illegitimate child, eight year old Thomas - and it will be remembered that she had begun her wisewoman career some ten years earlier - who was very soon to give damning evidence against her. And then there was the matter of the death of her brother Lawrence's wife. The two women had met each other on nearby Eliot's heath, a quarrel flared up and Ursula, beside herself with rage when she was called 'whore and witch', fell on her sister-in-law 'then took up her clothes and did beat her upon the hips and otherwise in words did misuse her greatly.'

Later that day, the unfortunate woman developed pains 'in her back and in the privy parts of her body.' This was hardly surprising, but she was convinced that she had had a spell put on her and took to her bed. As her husband was later to tell Darcy, she 'continued so a day and a night all the parts of her body cold like a dead creature's, and yet at her mouth did appear her breath to go and come'. She was in this state when Ursula came to her, without being sent for, lifted up her clothes and took her by the arm, 'the which she had not so soon done but straightaway after she gasped and never after drew her breath and so died.'

To Grace Thurlow this assault would have been a grotesque parody of the healing of her son and when, over the next three months, she was increasingly afflicted by 'a lameness in her bones, especially in her legs,' she did not put this down to a combination of rheumatic pains and the latter stages of her pregnancy but chose instead to believe that she too had, for some reason, offended Ursula Kemp and been bewitched.

In Elizabethan England, wisewomen often acted as midwives, using their traditional charms and herbal concoctions to help ease women in labour. However, the authorities, particularly the Church, tried to discourage this - in fact, licensed midwives had to swear an oath not to use 'any kind of sorcery or incantations in the time of travail of any woman' - but the practice was widespread, especially in rural areas. Given her concern for the boy's well-being, Ursula Kemp might well have fulfilled this rôle at the time of Davey's birth.

This time, however, Grace had asked someone else to be her midwife. She was actually in labour, surrounded by many of her neighbours, who would, as was customary, have gathered together to encourage her through the birth, when Ursula Kemp, having worked herself up into another of her rages, burst into the room, demanding to know why 'she had not the keeping in of her.'

Trying to keep the peace, Grace replied simply that 'she was provided' but the intruder, oblivious of her audience, who were no doubt lapping up every moment of this disgraceful scene, launched herself into another tirade. This time, Grace responded darkly that 'if she should continue lame as she had done before, she would find the means to know how it came and would creep upon her knees to complain of them to have justice done upon them.'

When this thinly veiled threat was shrugged off with a careless, 'That would be a good turn', Grace warned her, 'Take heed, Ursula, thou hast a naughty name' - with naughty at this time having, of course, the much stronger sense of evil or wicked.

Biting back her jealousy, Ursula forced herself to calm down. 'I cannot witch,' she assured her former friend, 'but I can unwitch, and if you will send for me privily and send your keeper away, I will show you how you can unwitch yourself, or any other at any time.'

But all this was to no avail, and after the baby - a girl - was born, Ursula's humiliation was complete when its mother refused to let her act as wet nurse when she returned to work in Lord Darcy's household at the Priory. Again, she might well have acted as nurse to Davey, but it was widely believed that an infant absorbed its nurse's morals - or lack of them - together with her milk, and Grace was not prepared to risk her baby being contaminated by any occult powers.

Despite this further rebuff, Ursula Kemp made one final attempt to get back into favour. The lameness in Grace's bones had indeed persisted and 'unsent for and without request' she came to her once more with a promise to help, not simply out of friendship now, but in return for a payment of twelve pence. This was agreed, and for five weeks the pains disappeared. When, however, the fee was demanded Grace whined 'that she was a poor and needy woman and had no money.' Payment in kind then, in the form of cheese, was suggested, but she rejected this too, claiming that she did not have any.

Given that she must have been constantly teetering on the very edge of poverty, it is hardly surprising that Ursula 'fell out with her and threatened to be even with her' - and even less surprising that Grace was straightaway 'taken lame, and from that day to this day hath so continued.' Davey's symptoms also returned, so that 'when she is anything well or beginneth to amend, then her child is tormented, and when he beginneth to amend then she becometh lame, so that without help she is not able to arise or to turn her in her bed.'

Even this, though - at least, according to her account - was nothing alongside the vengeance that Ursula Kemp now went on to exact.

St Clere's Hall

CHAPTER THREE

The hall was silent once more, the only sound the logs hissing and crackling in the huge fireplace, as Grace Thurlow drew breath before making her final, most damning accusation, 'Some short time after that falling out,' she said, 'the child lying in the cradle, and not above a quarter old, fell out of the cradle and broke her neck and died.'

Practically every household at this time, however impoverished, had a carved wooden cradle, set on rockers which the mother or nurse would use to lull the child to sleep. Grace admitted that she was caring for the baby at the time of this tragedy, and one wonders whether she might have left it unattended so that in a crying fit - or a convulsive attack similar to her brother's - it had jolted the cradle from its rockers? Or was this something more sinister than simple neglect or accident? Infanticide - with the mother, already driven to distraction by her son's recurring fits and her own unremitting aches and pains, the most likely suspect?

Her quarrel with Ursula Kemp was by now common knowledge, so she had no difficulty in pointing the finger of suspicion in her direction. And Ursula, with careless bravado, made no effort to divert it. 'It makes no matter,' she said, when told of the child's death. 'She should have suffered me to have the keeping and nursing of it.'

●●●●●

Agnes Letherdall also had a story to tell of childish ailments and petty squabbles. In a community where money did not come easily, barter was a long-established alternative to cash.

However, when Ursula Kemp sent her son Thomas to ask for some scouring sand to clean her pots and pans in exchange for 'the dyeing of a pair of women's hose', Agnes refused, telling the boy for good measure that his mother was a 'naughty beast'.

Ursula was not therefore best pleased when she saw Agnes's daughter taking sand to another of her neighbours and, as the girl reported back to her mother, she 'murmured' against her. The folly of crossing a known witch showed itself within hours, when Agnes's one year old baby - also a girl, called Elizabeth - developed 'a great swelling in the bottom of the belly and other privy parts.'

Over the next few months the condition worsened until, just the previous week, the child's mother had finally made up her mind to confront its source. Ursula Kemp was at home, spinning wool with another woman, when she arrived with the child, saying that she had been to a local wisewoman who had told her that Ursula Kemp had bewitched it.

She was not a good liar though, and Ursula, calling on the other woman as her witness, retorted that she would 'lay her life' that she had not been to any such person. This was true, but as it was widely held that witches had the power to see into other people's minds, her scornful response could simply be taken as further evidence of her guilt.

Next morning, the child was even worse, so Agnes decided that she would indeed take her to Mother

Ratcliff, a wisewoman whom she had consulted on previous occasions. Having examined the child, the woman confirmed that she was bewitched, prescribed various remedies but warned that she could not hold out much hope for its recovery. To get to Mother Ratcliff's, Agnes, carrying the wailing baby in her arms, had to go by Ursula Kemp's house. 'Passing by the window, the infant cried to the mother, "Woe, woe," and pointed with the finger towards the window. And the child used the like as she passed homeward by the said window.' This was no doubt no more than a combination of wails and feeble struggles. But for Agnes this infantile percipience was enough to justify a second confrontation with her tormentor, who this time 'used such speeches as moved her to complain.'

The child was with Agnes in the courtroom and when it was now brought out and examined, it 'appeared to be in most piteous sort consumed, and the privy and hinder parts thereof to be in a most strange and wonderful case, as it seemed to every honest woman of good judgement, and not likely to live and continue any long time.' And in fact, just seven days later, it died.

Darcy was closely observing Ursula Kemp's reaction during this pitiful scene and now, before adjourning for the day, he tightened the screw one notch further. In the first recorded instance of the practice in Essex, three of the 'honest women' were deputed to take her into an ante-room, strip her naked and search her body for the 'witch's teat', the devil's mark whereby she would suckle her familiar spirits with her blood. Witches were popularly believed to possess such spirits - demons that carried out their commands but which in turn held ultimate power over their souls. These were very different though from the devils - the succubi and incubi, for example - with whom Continental witches were thought to practise their perverted acts. In England they usually took the form of small animals - toads, for instance, or dogs, cats, and ferrets, in other words, the kind of tame and semi-domesticated creatures that lonely and embittered women would have found in and around their houses and adopted as pets.

Although the ownership of such spirits was not made a punishable offence until the Witchcraft Act of 1604, Darcy was anxious to establish the presence of the teat on Ursula Kemp's body. Any mole or blemish could of course be readily identified as such, if that was what the searchers were looking for, and it was no surprise that the women solemnly reported back to him that they had indeed discovered several such marks. So, the accused possessed at least one demonic spirit, probably more - the perfect line for Darcy to pursue next day, when he would for the first time interrogate Ursula Kemp herself

CHAPTER FOUR

After consigning her to a no doubt sleepless night huddled in the bleak, windowless village lock-up - or 'cage' as it was popularly known, Darcy maintained the psychological pressure by keeping his prisoner waiting until late afternoon before finally summoning her to his presence. He then sprang his second surprise by immediately leading her from the great hall out into the garden where, with the February dusk closing round them they were alone. Perhaps he took her to his herb garden where, walking along gravelled paths among the low box hedges, she would have been surrounded by the plants - culinary and medicinal - that were so familiar to her. But if this did anything to allay her rising tension, it was merely a prelude to the next stage of his strategy.

After she had freely admitted her activities as a wise-woman he moved on to the charges and the damning evidence laid against her. He urged her to confess, assuring her that if she did so 'she should have great favour' - a promise he had not the slightest intention of keeping. 'You should be aware,' he added, 'that there is a man of great knowledge come over lately unto our Queen's Majesty, who has informed her of what a company and number of witches be within England.' This was none other than Jean Bodin, Darcy's continental mentor, but in fact his address before Elizabeth had made no mention of witchcraft, being concerned with the need for religious toleration, a cause that Bodin embraced despite his extreme views elsewhere.

The discouerie
of witchcraft,

Wherein the lewde dealing of witches.
and witchmongers is notablie detected, the
knauerie of coniurors, the impietie of inchan-
tors, the follie of soothsaiers, the impudent fals-
hood of cousenors, the infidelitie of atheists,
the pestilent practises of Pythonists, the
curiositie of figurecasters, the va-
nitie of dreamers, the beggerl-
lie art of Alcu-
mystrie,

The abhomination of idolatrie, the hor-
rible art of poisoning, the vertue and power of
naturall magike, and all the conueiances
of Legierdemaine and iuggling are deciphered:
and many other things opened, which
haue long lien hidden, howbeit
verie necessarie to
be knowne.

Heerevnto is added a treatise vpon the
nature and substance of spirits and diuels,
&c: all latelie written
by Reginald Scot
Esquire.

1. Iohn 4, 1.

Beleeue not euerie spirit, but trie the spirits, whether they are
of God; for manie false prophets are gone
out into the world, &c.
1584

Such a minor point was not going to deter Darcy. 'Whereupon,' he went on, 'I and other of her Justices have received commission for the apprehending of as many as are within these limits, and they which do confess the truth of their doings, they shall have much favour. But as for the other, they shall be burned and hanged.'

Faced with this classic blend of apparent sympathy and brutal threats, Ursula, 'bursting out with weeping, fell upon her knees' and admitted that she did indeed possess demonic spirits. Two, called Titty and Jack, were male, taking the forms of grey and black cats, and they had the power to kill her enemies, whilst the other two, Pigin, in the shape of a black toad, and Tyffin, 'like a white lamb', were female and could inflict lameness and other bodily ailments and could also be used to destroy cattle.

The urge to confess to incredible crimes is a recurring psychological phenomenon, still present today. It was certainly widespread at that time among those accused of witchcraft. As Reginald Scot put it: 'The witch, expecting her neighbours' mischances, and seeing things sometimes come to pass according to her wishes, curses and incantations, confesseth that she (as a goddess) hath brought such things to pass.'

Ursula Kemp is a case in point and, at least according to Darcy, she went on 'without any asking and of her own free will' to admit that she had sent her spirits to torment Agnes Letherdall's child, kill her sister-in-law and overturn the Thurlow child's cradle. Darcy had the breakthrough he was seeking, but it was essential for these admissions to be made before witnesses. So, after adjourning for

St Osyth lock-up as it is today, complete with plaque and a bedroom extension above

what he no doubt considered a well-earned supper, he reconvened the hearing and the accused repeated her confession, tearfully begging forgiveness from her victims.

Then, just when Darcy must have thought his day was complete, she went on to accuse her neighbour, Alice Newman, of actually sending the spirits to torment the two women. Darcy wasted no time; a warrant was issued summoning Alice Newman to appear before him the next day.

Before he could begin questioning her though, Ursula, after another night in the lock-up, declared that she had more to tell him. Some four months previously, she and her neighbour had fallen out, with Alice accusing her of being a witch and threatening to inform Brian Darcy, but they had then made up their quarrel and the woman had taken all four spirits away with her to her house. It was from here that they had been sent on their lethal missions, although on their return they had first reported back to her and were rewarded by sucking her blood before going back to their new mistress.

Alice Newman confirmed the first part of this story, but resolutely denied that she had taken possession of the spirits. Darcy responded that if she did not confess, the spirits would be taken from her, by force if necessary.

'Oh no, you will not,' came the defiant response. 'I shall hold them tightly to me.' Then seeing the trap she had blundered into, she added lamely, 'That is, if I had any.'

But she was too late. The floodgates were open and after a third night in gaol a torrent of admissions and accusations flowed from Ursula Kemp. John Stratton's wife Edena had refused to give her spices so the black cat spirit, Jack, had tormented her and her child and she had died just a week previously.

Alice Newman had quarrelled with John Butler, and her spirit had afflicted him with pains in his back; and it was after Johnson, who under the Poor Law Act of 1579 had been appointed Collector for the Poor by Darcy, had rejected Alice's request for twelve pence, claiming that he had already disbursed more money than he had taken in, that she had bewitched both him and his wife to death.

Ursula knew all this because Tyffin, her white lamb, had told her so, and it was also Tyffin who informed her about three more of her neighbours. Agnes Glascock had put a death spell on Mitchell the shoemaker's child, and also the illegitimate child being cared for by Page and his wife - the very woman who, in her wisewoman role, Ursula had cured of lameness. Elizabeth Bennet had two spirits, one in the shape of a black dog called Suckin, and Lyerd, which was red (presumably russet-brown) 'like a lion'. One day she had looked in at the other woman's window and seen a third spirit 'lift up a cloth lying over a pot, looking much like a ferret.' It does not seem to have occurred to her that this might have been because the creature really was a ferret!

Suckin and Lyerd between them had tormented two local women and a child, inflicted a fatal abscess on a man called Willinghall and plagued William Willes's wife 'whereof she languished many years and died.' Two of William Byett's cows were killed, whilst a third had only

just been saved. Having given it up for dead, the farmer
had lit a fire of straw round it and was about to finish it
off with a blow of his axe to the head when the heat
roused the beast from the spell she was under and she
had sprung to her feet and lumbered off. But then, two
weeks before, Byett himself and his wife Joan had died.

Ursula Kemp declared that she had also seen another
ferret-like spirit in the house of another neighbour, Alice,
the wife of William Hunt, a mason. When she asked
Tyffin what it had done, she was told that on 1st January
that year it had caused the deaths of six cattle on William
Hayward's farm at Frowick, a mile from St Osyth on the
Colchester road.

Darcy of course made no attempt to disprove or
ridicule the garrulous lamb/spirit stories, merely asking his
prisoner if it had ever told her any lies.

'Oh no,' she assured him. 'I have never known it tell
me anything but the truth.'

Warrants were immediately issued for the detention
of the other three women, with Elizabeth Bennet the first
to be brought before him. She began by denying 'with
many oaths' any knowledge of the spirits or the earthen-
ware pot lined with wool where she supposedly kept them.
So Darcy put it to her that if it could be proved that she
did indeed possess such a pot, would she then accept that
all the other accusations were true? The pot was duly
produced and she admitted that it was hers but denied
ever seeing the woollen lining before.

Darcy therefore took her out into the garden, where
he repeated the ploy which had already worked so well

with Ursula Kemp, and once again a tearful confession came tumbling out. Yes, she said, she did own the spirits called Suckin and Lyerd, but they had forced themselves on her. Over the past two years she had suffered a number of seizures which had temporarily paralysed her - on one occasion she had, as a result, badly burned her arm whilst stirring the fire in her oven - and each time the spirits had been nearby.

She had managed to fight them off by praying to God and the Trinity, but another time, when she was milking, they came and sat on each side of her, with Suckin in his usual form of a black dog and Lyerd in the shape of a hare. All at once the cow gave a loud snort and ran off, knocking over the pail and spilling the milk so that her husband John 'did much chide her'.

She admitted that she had quarrelled with Byett and when the farmer had cursed her and her cattle she had turned the spell back on him by retorting, 'Wind it up, Byett, for it will light upon yourself.' She also agreed that she had been angry with his wife after she had killed one of her pigs with a pitchfork, with the result that Henry Durrant, the butcher, had refused to buy it from her, but she claimed that her spirits had tormented the two of them to death of their own accord, in order to gain favour with her - a claim that of course cut little ice with Darcy.

Next to face him was Agnes Glascock, who had a strange tale to tell of poltergeists and things going bump in the night. Many years previously, when she was aged about twenty, she was living with her brother Edward and a boarder called Arnold. On several occasions mysterious rumblings were heard in the roof, and lead weights and large stones came hurtling into the house, always uncomfortably close to their lodger. The man's wife already had a reputation as a witch and, being jealous of the young Agnes, was clearly trying to drive him from temptation. Soon after this, Agnes herself developed nagging aches in her bones and travelled to Sudbury to consult a wise-man named Herring. After confirming that Arnold's wife had bewitched her, he gave her a small linen bag 'of the breadth of a groat' containing what seemed to be tiny seeds. She had to sew this into her dress near where the pains were, and the symptoms quickly disappeared.

She had therefore had first-hand experience of magic, but was adamant that she had never harmed either Mitchell's or Page's children. Darcy, however, had her searched by, among others, Agnes Letherdall, who was hardly the most impartial of witnesses and, sure enough, the tell-tale marks were found on her left thigh and shoulder. He then brought her face to face with Ursula Kemp, who repeated her accusations, adding for good measure that she had bewitched a third child.

Agnes fell into a rage, calling her whore and threatening to scratch her - another traditional means of warding off a witch's powers - for she was certain that a spell had been put on her because she could no longer weep.

Next to take the stand was Alice Hunt. Nine years previously she had appeared before the Chelmsford Assize and been accused, but acquitted, of practising witchcraft.

Moreover, her mother, Mother Barnes, who had died less than two weeks ago, was widely regarded as a notorious witch. However, she too denied Ursula Kemp's allegations. Darcy was on the point of committing her into custody when she said that she wished to speak with him alone. So, for the third time, he led the way into the garden and here she immediately fell to her knees and admitted that until six days previously she had owned two spirits, called Robin and Jack, who had told her of Ursula Kemp's arrest and warned that she would be betrayed, then they had fled, telling her 'to shift for herself.'

Her sister, Margery Sammon, also had two spirits, she said, in the shape of toads, and all four demons had been given to them by their mother. Margery was immediately arrested and, after a night in the lock-up, brought before Darcy.

She agreed that she had watched over her mother on her deathbed but denied all knowledge of any spirits. However, her sister stuck to her story and when Margery continued to protest her innocence Alice drew her to one side, whispering in her ear.

Whatever she said, it was enough for the woman to break down and admit that her mother had indeed bequeathed the two spirits to her, but had told her that if she did not want them she should pass them on to Mother Pechey, 'for I know she is a witch and will be glad of them.'

When she heard of Ursula Kemp's arrest she too panicked and ordered the spirits to leave her, sending them on their way with the words, 'All evil go with you, and the Lord in Heaven bless me from you.' The last she saw of them they were heading towards a barred stile in Howe Lane, which led directly to Mother Pechey's house.

Joan Pechey, who was well over sixty, had lived in St Osyth all her adult life. Alice Hunt was her next-door neighbour, with just a wattle and daub wall between them, and she now told Darcy of how she had often overheard the old woman swearing and cursing. In particular, she had heard her muttering imprecations against Johnson after the Collector had given her bread that, perhaps with her toothless gums, was too hard-baked to eat.

'Yea, are you so saucy?' she had said. 'Are you so bold? You were not best to be so bold with me, for if you will not be ruled you shall have Symond's sauce.'

M R Tilley's definitive *A Dictionary of Proverbs in England in the Sixteenth and Seventeenth Centuries* cites 1640 as the first recorded reference to Symond's or Simondsall sauce: 'To denote a guest bringing an hungry appetite to our table or when a man eats little, to say he wants some of Simondsall sauce.' In other words, a hearty appetite, not to say greed, does not require the addition of a highly-spiced sauce. Nearly sixty years earlier, Joan Pechey was using the saying, with enough wit to make a pun on sauce/saucy in order to imply that Johnson was both impudent and greedy.

She had not yet finished berating him though. 'Yea,' she went on, 'I perceive that if I do give you an inch you will take an ell' - an ell being an Elizabethan measurement, particularly for cloth, of just over a yard.

A variation of this common saying was 'Give a knave an inch, he'll take an ell', and, even though the old woman's anger seems to have befuddled her, she is clearly reviling the man for what she sees as his selfish, grasping nature.

Mother Pechey was alone at the time and so, with no thought that the woman might, as usual, have simply been grumbling to herself, Alice had no doubt that she was speaking to her spirits. When, shortly afterwards, both Johnson and his wife died, there could be only one explanation. Margery Sammon backed up this story, saying that her sister had told her what she had heard. This was of course entirely hearsay, but Darcy saw no problem in admitting it as evidence.

Inevitably, Joan Pechey was the next to be summoned but here at last Darcy met his match. She fiercely denied having any spirits, whether from Margery Sammon or anyone else. He asked if she owned a cat (the most common of all such spirits) and she admitted that she had a kitten and a little dog, but when he enquired as to the colour of the kitten she retorted that if he wanted to know he could go and see for himself. She also denied cursing Johnson and she met the question of what she thought of the Collector's unexpected death with the bland remark that 'he was a very honest man and died very suddenly.'

Darcy was not going to give up so easily though, and he tried another tack. Witches were notorious for their sexual perversions, so he next raised the matter of the local gossip concerning herself and her twenty-three year old son Phillip. Once again she strenuously denied any wrong-doing, but when the young man was called to the witness stand he declared that 'many times and of late he hath lain in naked bed with his own mother, being willed and commanded so to do of her.'

Two much younger children then gave testimony against their own mothers. Ursula Kemp's eight year old son Thomas spoke of how he had seen her feeding her four spirits with beer, together with bread or cake, adding that they had then sucked her blood, whilst Alice Hunt's daughter Phoebe, who was also aged eight, said that her mother had fed her demons with milk before sending them to Hayward's farm at Frowick.

Finally, Darcy heard evidence from three more townsmen. John Tendering described the miraculous recovery of Byett's cow; William Hook, a painter and next-door neighbour of Alice Newman, told of the quarrels he had overheard between her and her husband over the spirits she reputedly kept in their house; and William Bonner claimed that just ten days previously Elizabeth Bennet had put a spell on his wife so that her upper lip was swollen and her eyes were sunk in her head.

So, at the end of seven days of charge and counter-charge, abject confessions and vehement denials, Darcy was satisfied that he had gathered sufficient testimony to consign all five women to the gaol in Colchester Castle, where they would remain until their cases were heard at the next Assize.

CHAPTER FIVE

News of Darcy's success spread rapidly throughout the surrounding district and people saw their chance to rid themselves of long-suspected witches from their own localities. Within three days, he began hearing testimony against a husband and wife from the village of Little Clacton, some four miles from St Osyth.

A farmer, Richard Ross, was the first to give evidence. Harking back six years, he told how he and Henry Sellis had often worked together on their neighbouring farms. On this occasion, however, while Sellis was ploughing with two of his horses, 'they being as well and as likely to any man's judgement', they both suddenly dropped dead. It was only then that Ross recalled that shortly before this he had refused to sell two bushels of malt to Sellis's wife Cicely 'which she would have had for three shillings but he held at ten groats.' Three shillings were the equivalent of nine groats, but this difference of a single groat, or fourpence, was enough to spark a quarrel between them.

He could ill afford the loss of two fine horses, but other misfortunes soon followed. His wife found their neighbours' cattle straying onto their land and drove them off, at which Cicely Sellis 'was in great anger and gave her lewd speeches.' Within a very short time, many of his beasts suffered a mysterious sickness, and he was convinced that this had been 'wrought by some witchcraft or sorcery by the said Henry or Cicely his wife.' Then, six months ago, his barn, filled with corn, caught fire for no apparent reason. This time he could not in all honesty

Witches flying on broomsticks from a witch's house to a sabbat. From *Witchcraft, Magic and Alchemy*, by Gillot de Givry, 1579

accuse his neighbours, except that he had overheard John, their six year old son, say, 'Here is a goodly deal of corn' and a man's voice that he could not identify had replied, 'Yes, it is the devil's store.'

John had an older brother, Henry, aged nine, and Darcy now took evidence from the two boys. They both told a similar tale of how, just the previous month, at about midnight a spirit came and grabbed hold of the younger boy's left leg and little toe. His leg was still bruised and the toenail broken. Except that it was black, this spirit was very like their sister - perhaps because in reality it was her, playing a childish prank. In any case, the terrified boy called out to his father who turned on their mother, saying, 'You stinking whore, cannot you keep your imps away from my children?'

The older boy declared that his mother had two spirits, living under a crab apple tree by their house. One, a male, was black and called Hercules, while the other was a white female named Mercury. His brother confirmed this but added that just recently - perhaps getting wind of events in the neighbouring parish - his father had told her to send them away or kill them. She had given them to a man from Colchester. He was not sure of his name but it was either Weedon or Glascock. However, Darcy does not seem to have followed up any possible connection with Agnes Glascock from St Osyth.

Henry ended his evidence by naïvely saying that on their way to the courtroom that morning his mother had told him, 'Take heed ye say nothing.' In fact though he and his brother had said more than enough for Darcy to move on now to the parents themselves. Henry Sellis confirmed Richard Ross's tale of the plough horses but claimed to have no recollection of any quarrel over malt, whilst Cicely said that she could not remember any dispute with Ross's wife. Both of them also utterly refuted their sons' stories about the black spirit and its midnight assault. Undeterred, Darcy ordered three women to examine Cicely and, inevitably, they discovered on her body 'many spots very suspicious' - very similar, in fact, to those they had found on the St Osyth women.

One of the searchers was Joan Smith, who now took the stand to tell how one Sunday a few months earlier she was going to church, carrying her young child in her arms, when she met her mother and two other women, one of whom was Cicely Sellis. The grandmother cooed over the baby, saying, 'Ah, Mother Pugs, art thou coming to church?' and the second woman joined in with, 'Here's a pretty and likely child, God bless it.' Cicely though shattered this mood, saying darkly, 'She only has the one child, just a little babe to play with for a time', and soon after this the child fell ill and died. Despite this pathetic story, Joan Smith was determined to be fair to the woman standing before her.

'My conscience,' she declared, 'will not let me charge Cicely or her husband to be the causers of any such matter. But I pray to God to forgive them if they have dealt in this way.'

The aptly named Thomas Death was not so circumspect. Like Ursula Kemp, Cicely Sellis at times took on the nursing of her neighbours' children, but two years previously a baby was taken out of her care and handed over to his wife. When the two women next met Cicely 'chid and railed at her, saying, 'Thou shalt lose more by the having of it than thou shalt have for the keeping of it." Within a month, several of his pigs, a calf and - far worse - their four year old son John were all dead. Death was a sailor and soon after this tragedy he went to sea again, eventually landing in Ipswich. Here he met by chance a messenger from home who told him that his other child, Mary, was seriously ill. The man had with him a sample of the girl's urine which he was taking to a physician in the town, hoping that he could diagnose what was wrong with her. Death of course went with him and asked if his daughter was bewitched, but the doctor refused to commit himself, fearful of dabbling in such dangerous waters.

Not satisfied with this, Death took the urine instead to a wiseman - he either could not or would not remember his name - who told him that he had come just in time to save the girl. Within two nights, the man said, those who had harmed his daughter would appear before her and she would be cured. The wiseman also gave him various remedies and, because he had to rejoin his ship, Death sent these back with the messenger.

When he at last came home again, his wife told him that the very next night after Mary had begun taking the medicines she had heard a loud groaning at about midnight and when she went to investigate the girl said, 'If you had come sooner you would have seen Cicely Sellis and Barker's wife here standing before me.'

Mary Death confirmed her mother's story. She had been suffering from a numbness stretching from her neck all down her back so that it took two or three people to turn her over in bed. On this particular night she had heard a voice telling her to look up, and when she did so she saw the two women 'standing before her in the same apparel that they usually wear.' They told her not to be afraid then vanished and by the next morning she was well enough to get out of bed unaided.

The girl would obviously have been aware that Cicely Sellis had been blamed for her brother's death - he had fallen down lifeless in their yard, been revived but then died - so she could well have been almost literally haunted by thoughts of the woman as she lay on what was so nearly her own deathbed. And of course the messenger had probably passed on the wiseman's prophecy along with his remedies. Despite this, her story must have made a profound impression in the courtroom, reinforcing her listeners' view of Cicely Sellis as a dealer in the occult.

Richard Ross's servant, Alice Baxter, had suffered from a kind of paralysis. One afternoon some four months previously she was in a field milking her master's cows. She was with the last when it suddenly gave a start knocking over the pail, and she saw that all the other cows were looking about them in a strange manner. She went on milking but all at once felt a sharp pain in her right side, as if someone had hit her. As she was carrying the milk back to the farm 'there came a thing all white like a cat and struck her at the heart so that she could not stand, go nor speak, and so she remained until her master, who she did not know when he came unto her, and two of his workmen did carry her home in a chair.'

She eventually emerged from this catatonic state but her terrifying experience was naturally seen as yet another sign of the malevolent workings of witchcraft. This view was damningly reinforced by young Henry Sellis, when he told the court that he had heard his mother tell his father that she had sent her spirit Hercules to Ross's maid and he had replied that she was 'a trim fool'. Hercules was supposedly a black spirit and Alice had seen a white cat, but Darcy of course chose to ignore such a minor discrepancy. Certainly, he was confident that he had heard enough to justify despatching Cicely Sellis and her husband to join their fellow accused in Colchester Gaol.

By this time, the prisoners, crowded together in just two small, foul-smelling cells and with irons attached to their ankles, had become something of a public spectacle. Henry Durrant, the butcher who had refused to buy Elizabeth Bennet's pig, reported back to Darcy after he and several villagers had visited the castle 'to see the witches that were committed thither.' He took the opportunity to speak to Ursula Kemp and she confirmed what he had long suspected - that his daughter Rebecca had had a death spell put on her by Alice Hunt and her mother, Widow Barnes. They had done this, said Ursula, because he had at one time refused to sell them a piece of pork, and he then recalled the occasion when he had sent them away empty-handed because the meat was 'newly dressed and he would not cut it out.'

Presumably with this further allegation, Ursula Kemp was still seeking that elusive 'favour' which Darcy had promised her. For the same reason, perhaps, she sent word that she wished to speak with him again, so he and Thomas Tey, a fellow Justice of the Peace, came to the gaol. Here she informed them that her spirit Tyffin had told her that Alice Newman had sent one of her spirits to plague his kinsman, the late Lord Darcy, to death.

Darcy may or may not have believed her - or perhaps he was restrained by the scepticism of his colleague - but this allegation does not appear on the final charge sheet that he drew up. However, the story was at least one more contribution to the atmosphere of superstition and fear that was now threatening to engulf the entire area.

The thirteenth century cells of Colchester Castle, where Darcy's victims were confined

CHAPTER SIX

Darcy was still taking evidence against Henry and Cicely Sellis when, on the thirteenth of March, he began hearing allegations concerning three women from Thorpe-le-Soken, whose inhabitants seized the opportunity to settle old scores, dredging to the surface events from many years past. Phyllis Okey, for instance, told how her late husband had once stumbled into a bramble bush, badly scratching his face, and was convinced to his dying day that their neighbour, Elizabeth Eustace, had brought this about because his wife had driven the woman's geese off their land, accidentally hurting one in the process.

Robert Sannevet had also incurred Elizabeth Eustace's anger. Fifteen years previously her daughter was working for him as a maidservant but he had had occasion to reprimand her 'for some lewd dealings and behaviour.' The girl's mother took offence at this, and the very next day 'as he was sitting by his fireside, his mouth was drawn awry, well near up to the upper part of his cheek.' He sent for a healer who, after advising him to dismiss the girl, freed the spasm by covering his eyes with a linen cloth and striking him hard on the cheek.

The ill-feeling between himself and Mother Eustace had persisted and when, three years ago, his brother 'was taken very sickly and at times was without any remembrance' he blamed her, saying that he would like to see a red hot spit thrust into her buttocks. These hasty words found their way to the woman and when, shortly afterwards, his wife gave birth to a still-born child he had no doubt who was to blame. The following summer, the milk from his cows became contaminated with blood - a sure sign to the modern farmer of mastitis. Then in the autumn many of his pigs began to skip and leap about his yard, in a manner horribly reminiscent of today's BSE in cattle, before they died.

One of Thorpe's constables, John Sayer, had also suffered from a paralysing spasm, but in his case it was his cart that was bewitched. He was passing Alice Manfield's house when, on firm, dry ground, it stuck fast for over an hour. He and several other men struggled to lift up the wheels before fixing a rope to drag it free but this snapped, as did the horse's harness. Then he remembered that a few days earlier a thatcher had been repairing his barn when Mother Manfield came and asked him if he would thatch a roof over her oven. The man replied that he would if Sayer allowed him to, but this was not good enough for the old woman - she was aged sixty-three 'or thereabouts' - and angry words passed between them.

When Darcy questioned her, she willingly confirmed the constable's story but corrected him in one respect. The reason she had bewitched his cart was that he had been transporting dung and had spilled some right outside her door! A spirit named Puppet had carried out this spell for her and she had rewarded it with a drink of beer.

Altogether, she said, she had four spirits, two male and two female, all in the shape of black cats. But, she added, they did not actually belong to her. Some twelve years before, Margaret Grevell had told her that she was going to live in another part of the village and did not want anyone to see her imps while she was making the move. So she agreed to keep them in her house, with her former neighbour being able to make use of them whenever she wished. And over the years, that was precisely what she had done, sending them off to spoil brewings of beer and batches of bread, to lame and kill animals and people - and even bewitch her own husband to death. The previous autumn they had been sent to Little Clacton to stay with Cicely Sellis for a week, and had made the most of their vacation by setting fire to Richard Ross's barn. She had not, stressed Alice, instigated any of these missions but the spirits told her about them on their return and she rewarded them with beer and bread, while their owner suckled them with her blood.

Then, just a week ago, one of the spirits warned her of her imminent arrest and said that they were going to St Osyth, either to Ursula Kemp or Mother Barnes's daughters. Their supernatural powers presumably did not extend to informing them that their seven-mile journey would be wasted because all three women were by then behind bars in Colchester Gaol! Even so, this, together with the reference to Ross's barn, shows that some of the accused from the various localities were known to each other, if only by reputation.

There is no sign though of any conscious linking together, whether in a coven or any other grouping. In Scotland there is ample evidence of this with, for example, the North Berwick witches, under the direction of a local schoolmaster, Doctor John Fian, being accused in 1591 of conspiring together to create the storm that nearly drowned King James VI and his bride, Anne of Denmark. James was present at the trial and seems to have personally instigated the 'strange torment' - as the contemporary pamphlet *News From Scotland* puts it - that was inflicted on the unfortunate Fian. All his finger nails were torn off with pincers and in their place needles were thrust in even up to their heads.' When this failed to produce a confession, he was subjected to the 'torment of the boots' whereby 'his legs were crushed and beaten together as small as might be, and the bones and flesh so bruised that the blood and marrow spouted forth in great abundance, whereby they were made unserviceable for ever.' This, in a sense, was irrelevant, for Fian did now admit his guilt and was duly burned.

However, there is no hint of such organization in England. The one possible exception is the group of thirty-five 'witches', drawn mainly from two families from the Pendle area in Lancashire, who in 1612 supposedly plotted to kill the gaoler of Lancaster Prison by blowing up the castle, but this is an isolated example.

Having done her best to divert attention away from herself, Alice Manfield now turned on Elizabeth Eustace, claiming that she had been to her house and seen three spirits looking like cats, one white, one grey and one black, and that one of them had told her that their mistress had sent them to harm a child.

This stream of allegations was made before the constables from Thorpe and many of her fellow villagers, and when it finally came to an end Darcy solemnly warned her 'what a danger it was, and how highly she should offend God if she should charge any person with anything untrue.' But when, in the presence of the two women she had accused, her statement was read back to her she reaffirmed the truth of every word.

They, of course, denied this and, in any case, it was now her turn to be accused with more people pressing forward to tell of occasions when they had fallen foul of her. Joan Cheston had rejected her request for curds and shortly afterwards her cattle fell lame so that for eight days they could not walk to the pasture and she had had to use some of her precious winter fodder to keep them alive. Another woman, the wife of a man called Lynd, said that Mother Manfield had once asked her for some milk and she had replied that she had none to spare, having barely enough to suckle her new-born calf - and that very night the calf died.

All of this evidence was heard in a single day and Darcy concluded a highly satisfactory session by consigning all three women to Colchester Gaol. When, however, he visited them there a few days later Margaret Grevell and Elizabeth Eustace again asserted their innocence, and although the former was searched no suspicious marks were found on her body. This though was not enough for her to be freed, especially as in the meantime two more men from Thorpe had come forward with fresh allegations against her.

John Carter claimed that shortly after a falling out between them, he had failed in three attempts to brew his beer properly. Finally, his son had tried the age-old remedy of firing an arrow into the liquid. His first two shots missed but the third - making a second magical three - hit its target and the brewing was then completed successfully.

The village butcher, Nicholas Strickland, was also certain that he had suffered at her hands. He had refused to sell her a rack of mutton because he had not finished preparing it. A few days afterwards, milk that his wife was simmering turned sour, and later that same week she spent from early morning till ten at night struggling to churn cream into butter. She tried again the next day but in the end had to admit defeat and it was poured into the swill tub.

This evidence was given on March the twentieth, by which time Darcy's net had spread even further, trawling up from the murky depths of village life stories of petty quarrels, vengeance - and murder.

CHAPTER SEVEN

For many years, Agnes Herd's sharp tongue and hasty temper had led her into disputes with her fellow-villagers in Little Oakley. She had also fallen foul of the church authorities and when she received Darcy's summons she was already waiting to appear before the ecclesiastical court in Colchester, accused of being a witch. If found guilty, she would either have to perform a public penance, confessing her sins in church, or might even be excommunicated, but she could escape punishment if she could persuade enough individuals to speak on her behalf

However, when she approached her neighbour John Wade he refused to help her - which was hardly surprising because he was one of those who had 'presented' her name to the diocesan authorities. She went off in a huff, saying she would ask a man named John Aldust from nearby Ramsey instead. But for John Wade this was not to be the end of the matter.

He kept a flock of sheep on an eighty-acre pasture at Tendring, employing a local man to look after them, and when, after an absence of a week or so, he went to see how they were he discovered that four had died and others were in a very sorry state. Things went from bad to worse, and over the next two months no fewer than twenty sheep and lambs, together with several of his cows, with a total value of four pounds, either died or fell lame.

Thomas Cartwright had also clashed with Agnes Herd. Three winters previously, after a large bough from one of his trees had blown down in a blizzard, she broke off a piece and laid it over a patch of mud outside her house. Unaware of this, he took it home with him, and when she found out what he had done she told a neighbour that she would be even with him. Just three nights later, during another snow storm, his best cow fell into a ditch and broke its neck. During that same night another cow died whilst giving birth - and of course both mishaps were laid at the door of 'some witchery of the said Agnes Herd.'

More and more villagers added their voices and their stories give sad yet vivid glimpses into a stratum of society clinging desperately to the very edges of survival where the most minor of misfortunes could all too easily turn into a major tragedy.

Bennet Lane, married now but at the time a widow, gave Agnes Herd a pint of milk 'and also loaned her a dish to bear it home, the which dish she kept a fortnight or three weeks'. In the end she had to ask for it back and Agnes's daughter brought it to her. She was spinning at the time but all at once the thread broke and kept on snapping. She tried sharpening the spindle on her grind-stone but this did no good, and it was only when she put it into the fire, making it red hot, that she was able to get on with her work.

On another occasion, Agnes Herd owed her two pence and she had to ask for it because her church tithe was due. This was an annual payment, based on a tenth of her paltry income, and failure to pay on time could result in a summons to the spiritual court.

Agnes said that she did not have the money and would let her have it the following week, but this would be too late. 'You must needs let me have it now,' Bennet urged, 'for this day I must pay the Lord's rent.' So the disgruntled woman went off and borrowed the tuppence a second time in order to repay her.

In return, Bennet gave her another pint of milk, but next day, when she was making cream her milk turned sour and foul-smelling. At first she thought this was because she had been feeding her animals from the utensils, 'whereupon she scalded her vessels and scoured them with salt, thinking that might help, but it was never the better but as before, and she was full of care that she should lose both milk and cream.'

It was only when she tried putting a red-hot horseshoe into the liquid that she could seethe her milk, fleet her cream and make her butter' as well as she always did. Ever since men first began working in metal, especially iron, it was thought to have magical qualities, and by the sixteenth century this was a tried and tested means of combating witchcraft. George Gifford, vicar of All Saints, Maldon, who continued to live in Essex until his death in 1620, refers to this belief in his *A Dialogue Concerning Witches and Witcheraftes*, published just a year after the St Osyth proceedings. The book takes the form of a conversation between a sceptic and a believer in the power of magic, and when told of this particular practice, the former asks, 'You do not know that the witch was in your cream, do you?'

'Some think she is there,' comes the reply, 'and therefore when they thrust in the spit they say, If thou beest here have at thee, aye.'

Although Agnes Herd seems to have been very much an outcast within her own community, some people at least took pity on her. One day she came begging to farmer Andrew West's house, saying that she had been to the mill but could get neither bread nor meal, and 'knowing her need he caused his wife to give her a piece of a loaf.' But he could not resist adding sternly, 'Agnes, thou art ill thought of for witchcraft', a charge that she strongly denied.

West's wife Anne then went on to tell her that they had just had a litter of pigs and would not be able to keep them all. 'I would somebody had one or two of them,' she said, and Agnes replied that although she could not afford to buy any 'if her landlord would give her leave to keep one, she wished that she would give her one.' This was agreed but when she did not come for it they thought she had changed her mind and sold the two pigs to a man called Penly. So when, a couple of days later, Agnes arrived to collect her pig, it was too late.

The following day. while a group of women were weeding their field, Anne West sent her nephew to Agnes with a pound of wool for her to spin. 'Can she not have her weeders to spin it?' she grumbled. 'Your aunt might as well have given me one of her pigs as to Penly.' This was duly reported back and within two hours one of their best pigs started squealing 'and staggering as though it were lame in the hinder parts.' The weeders gathered round, some saying it should be burned while another said they just needed to cut off its ears and burn them. This was done and eventually the animal recovered.

Two days later the two women met in the village and the farmer's wife berated Agnes bitterly. 'Thou saidst the other day thou hast no skill in witchery,' she cried. 'But I will say thou hast an unhappy tongue.' After this, she had failure after failure when trying to brew beer and it was only after someone told her to put a hot iron into the mash that the problem was overcome.

Edmond Osborne and his wife Godlife also had trouble with their beer. Malt from Manningtree, some eight miles distant, had a high reputation both locally and nationally. The ale that it produced was the staple drink at the town's annual Whitsun Fair, prompting the saying: 'You shall have a slave eat more at a meal than ten of the guard; and drink more in two days than all Manningtree does at a Whitsun-ale.' The beverage was traditionally accompanied by an ox roasted whole, and in Act Two of *Henry IV, Part One* Prince Hal likens Falstaff to 'a roasted Manningtree ox, with the pudding in his belly.' So Osborne was delighted to obtain, just before Christmas, some fine Manningtree malt and he carried it home in triumph, saying, 'Good wife, let us have some good drink made of it.'

The first brewing went well, but then Godlife sent to Agnes Herd for three pence that she was owed for a peck of apples. But she replied that she could not repay it until the woman came and paid her for what she had spun. And, of course, when they went to brew a second time it was a disaster. Even the red-hot iron treatment failed and the stinking mash was only fit for pigs' swill.

Darcy's next witness was Agnes Herd's illegitimate

daughter, Agnes Dowsing, six years old - and not perhaps the brightest of children. Oh yes, she agreed happily, her mother had a great many spirits. Five were like blackbirds and they lived in a box lined with black and white wool, and in another box she kept six more. These were like cows, with short horns, but were about as big as rats. Her mother had given her one of these - it was black and white and called Crow - and she gave another to her brother. This one was reddish-brown and answered to the name of Donne. Her mother fed them on wheat, barley and oats, as well as bread and cheese, while the ones like cows ate straw and hay, and drank either water or beer. Sometimes the blackbirds gathered round her brother, twittering and tweeting so loudly that he would put them back in their box. When Darcy asked the crucial question, had she ever seen her mother suckling her spirits, she said that the birds had sucked from her own hands and her brother's legs.

'Can you show us where they sucked?'

'Oh yes.' Solemnly, the girl held out her hand. 'Here sucked a bird and here sucked a bird and here sucked a bird.'

The effect was rather spoilt though, when she was asked why two of the marks were almost identical and she replied, 'Oh, those are where I burned myself'.

●●●●●

For the previous sixteen years, Richard Harrison had been parish priest of the church of St Mary in Little Oakley. Through his patron, Lord Darcy, Harrison also held the living of nearby Beaumont, but he lived with his

Richard Harrison's church at Little Oakley, now a private residence

wife and five children in a house that she owned in the village. He now rose to speak, with a tale of superstition and terror, of impotent anger and utter pathos - and agonizing death.

Like many priests at this time, he augmented his meagre stipend by farming the parsonage land. The previous summer, while he was away in London, his wife was caring for a duck that was sitting on a batch of eggs under a cherry tree in their hedge.

When they hatched, the ducklings disappeared and she suspected that Agnes Herd, 'a light woman and a common harlot', had stolen them. But when she accosted her, Agnes denied all knowledge of the ducklings and angry words passed between them.

Soon afterwards, Harrison returned home and that night spent two or three hours reading, having told his wife to go off to bed ahead of him. All at once, he heard her cry out, 'Oh Lord, Lord, help me and keep me.'

When he ran to her bedside, she clutched at his hand, saying, 'Oh Lord, I am sore afraid and have been divers times but I would not tell you. I am in no doubt, husband, that yonder wicked harlot, Agnes Herd, doth bewitch me.'

'I pray you be content and think not so,' he entreated her, 'but trust in God and put your trust in him only and He will defend you from her and from the Devil himself also.' But his words had no effect and he begged her to shake off her fears, saying, 'What will the people say that I being a preacher should have my wife so weak in faith?'

The poor woman though was clearly in the grip of an

extreme psychosomatic condition and nothing he could say could free her from this. She remained in bed for two months, growing weaker all the while, until at last she implored him, 'I pray you, as ever there was love between us, seek some remedy for me against yonder wicked beast, for if I have no remedy she will utterly consume me.'

That same day he had climbed up into a plum tree and was picking the ripe fruit when Agnes Herd came by and asked him for some. For the distracted husband, this was the last straw.

'I am glad you are come, you vile strumpet,' he shouted down at her. 'I do think you have bewitched my wife and, as truly as God doth live, if I can perceive that she be troubled any more as she hath been I will not leave a whole bone about thee, and moreover I will seek to have thee hanged.'

With that, he began to come down out of the tree and she, not surprisingly, 'did suddenly depart from him without having any plums.'

His wife's condition continued to worsen though, so that she was 'at many times afraid both sleeping and waking.' Then one day she called him to her, saying, 'Husband, God bless you and your children, and God send you good friends for I must depart from you, for I am now utterly consumed by yonder wicked creature, Agnes Herd.'

Again and again over the next two days she repeated, 'Oh, Agnes Herd, Agnes Herd, she hath consumed me.' And with these appalling words on her lips, she died.

CHAPTER EIGHT

Edward Upcher and his wife had for some time suspected that the mysterious illness that was afflicting her had been brought about by witchcraft. So, when news of Darcy's campaign reached them they made the journey from their home in Walton-on-the-Naze to Colchester, where they sought out Ursula Kemp in her prison cell.

She confirmed their fears, identifying the culprit as a woman from their own village. She had a mole under one of her arms, one ear was smaller than the other, and in her yard was a large stack of wood. This description matched a certain Joan Robinson so they and six more of her fellow villagers hurried to St Osyth to denounce her.

Their allegations followed the now familiar pattern. One woman had refused to lend her a haymaking tool and that night there was a terrible storm, after which a cow miscarried and her goose eggs failed to hatch. Another woman would not sell her a cheese, and the very next day her horse and cart became stuck in Vicarage Pond.

Joan Robinson is in a different category from most of the other accused. She was married and not, it would seem, short of cash. She fell out with one person over money that she was owed, and on several occasions the dispute was about items that she wanted to buy. Alice Walter, for instance, was not prepared to sell her a pig - and shortly afterwards the sow would not let her new litter suck 'but did bite and fly at them as though she had been mad.'

Margery Carter told how, ten years earlier, her husband had refused to lease a pasture to the Robinsons, and a short time later two of their cows broke their necks. Then, just two years previously, Joan Robinson's husband had tried to buy an acre of land from them intending to build a house, but they did not want the pair as neighbours - and the following day 'a fair ambling mare' worth at least five pounds died.

Many of the allegations were trivial and the evidence insubstantial but this did not prevent Darcy from sending her off to Colchester to await her trial. His final act, on Saturday, 29th March, little more than five weeks since he had heard the first accusation against Ursula Kemp, was to complete the certificate of charges levelled against the thirteen individuals who were now confined in the Castle Gaol.

They were not to be held there for very much longer though, for on that very same day they were transferred to Chelmsford for the commencement of the Lent Assize. Joan Robinson, however, was not among them. Her higher status is confirmed by the fact that she was freed on bail and then discharged before the hearings began.

Her name does reappear in the Assize records some seven years later, in July, 1589, when she was one of the 'jury of matrons' appointed to examine two women found guilty of murder by witchcraft who had pleaded for clemency on the grounds that they were pregnant. The matrons returned a negative report on one, Alice Adcock, but found that the other, Avis Coney, was indeed pregnant. Both women appear on the gaol roll for the

Mother Agnes Waterhouse of Hatfield Peverel, aged 63, probably the first Englishwoman to be hanged for witchcraft in 1566

following July, so it would seem that, although Coney might have escaped the gallows, she did not receive any more lenient treatment than her fellow accused.

Henry Sellis was also freed on bail before the Assize began, and there is no mention in the records of Margery Sammon, so it is likely that she too was discharged. However, Sellis's wife Cecily, together with the other nine accused, were brought to trial. But now, instead of the semi-official shamelessly biased proceedings in St Clere's Hall, their cases would be heard by two of the most experienced - and worldly-wise - judges on the Home Circuit, John Southcote and Thomas Gawdy.

These two Queen's Bench justices had presided over the Chelmsford trial of 1579 when four women from Hatfield Peverel were charged with murder and the destruction of live-stock through witchcraft. One of the accused, Elizabeth Francis, would have been familiar to Southcote for she had appeared before him fourteen years previously and been sentenced to both a prison term and the pillory for supposedly bewitching a woman and young boy. It was also after this trial that Agnes Waterhouse achieved the dubious distinction of being the first person in England to be executed under the Witchcraft Act of 1563.

Listed along with them for the current Assize was an impressive array of Justices, including William Cecil, Lord Burghley, Philip Howard, Earl of Arundel, Robert Dudley, Earl of Leicester, and Edward de Vere, Earl of Oxford. Whether such luminaries were actually present is doubtful, but among the county dignitaries cited were

St Osyth waterfront

Brian Darcy's kinsman, Lord Darcy, and his older brother, Thomas. Darcy himself, as a local Justice of the Peace, might also have been expected to be present. He played a prominent part in most of the Assizes held at Brentwood, Braintree and Witham, as well as Chelmsford, from 1581 onwards, acting as Lord High Sheriff in 1586, and it is perhaps an indication of the official view of his activities that he was excluded from the current proceedings.

Furthermore, many of the charges that he listed were dropped before the trials even began. Elizabeth Bennet for example, despite her confessions to the bewitching of seven people, four of them to death, was only tried for the murders of William Byett and his wife. Even more surprisingly, Agnes Herd faced just one charge - the killing of John Wade's cow, sheep and lambs. She was not even called to account for the death of Richard Harrison's wife, and one wonders if the authorities found something suspect in his harrowing story which the credulous Darcy had failed to detect.

It is certainly the case that four years later Harrison found himself in the dock at the Chelmsford Assize of January, 1586, on a charge of grand larceny. He was accused of breaking into the enclosure of Thomas Ward at Mose. (Mosses Farm and Moze Cross today lie on the outskirts of Great Oakley, midway between his two parishes of Beaumont and Little Oakley) and stealing a sheep, worth five shillings. This was a capital offence and when the grand jury, together with no fewer than eight justices, found him guilty, he pleaded benefit of clergy.

This often-abused device, applicable to anyone - ordained or not - who could read Latin, enabled him to escape the gallows. He could, however, have been sentenced to a year's imprisonment and, although no record of this exists, he would certainly have been branded on his right thumb with the mark of a convicted felon. He does seem to have been ruined for it was in 1586 that the tenure of his two parishes was ended, whilst a further indication of his tragic decline following the death of his wife is that his accomplice in the theft was also named Richard Harrison. This could well have been his eldest son who, instead of following his father to university and on to one of the professions, is referred to as a 'labourer' and, moreover, a fugitive from justice, for he was 'still at large'.

The verdicts at the 1582 Assize were very much in line with the prevailing scepticism in the English legal system. Joan Pechey and Elizabeth Eustace were two more to be freed before the hearings began, whilst three others, Margaret Grevell, Alice Manfield and Alice Hunt joined Agnes Herd in being acquitted. Guilty verdicts were brought in against Agnes Glascock, on three charges of murder, and Cecily Sellis, for the killing of four year old John Death, but in each case the death sentence was commuted to a year's imprisonment.

Cecily was also accused of setting fire to Richard Ross's barn and destroying corn valued at one hundred marks (sixty-six pounds - a very large sum when you consider that a skilled goldsmith would earn no more than eight pounds a year) but was found not guilty. Her husband, Henry, faced the same charge at the August assize. Quite why his case was postponed is not clear, although at his trial a second arson attempt on the same property was alleged, supposedly on the thirty-first of March, just after he had been freed on bail. It was claimed that he had been helped by his son Robert, the older brother presumably of John and Henry, who had testified before Darcy. Whatever the reason, he too was found not guilty and released.

The three remaining women tried in March were all found guilty. Alice Newman was jointly accused with Ursula Kemp of killing Edena Stratton and the children of Agnes Letherdall and Grace Thurlow, and following the verdict remained in prison until 1588. She could count herself fortunate though for her fellow accused, together with Elizabeth Bennet, who pleaded guilty to the murders of the Byetts, were both, as the Gaol Delivery Roll puts it in its terse (and ungrammatical) Latin, '*cul modo iudicati & su p collum*', in other words, 'judged guilty and hanged by the neck.'

The lucky ones presumably returned to their homes - for most of them there was nowhere else to go. How they took up the threads of their lives alongside their accusers - and how the children who had so glibly betrayed them fared - can only be imagined. Some at least do not seem to have changed their ways. It is probable that the 'Margery Barnes of St Osyth, spinster' who was tried on a charge of murder by witchcraft in 1584 was in fact Margery Sammon, daughter of Mother Barnes. She was accused of possessing three 'imps or spirits', a mole named Piggin (as was Ursula Kemp's black

69

toad), a grey cat called Rusfott and a dog by the name of Dunfutt, which between July and October, 1583, she employed to bewitch to death John Lane. She was found not guilty but the woman who was charged with her, Joan Dale, also a spinster 'of St Osyth', fared less well for before the case came to trial she, like so many held on remand, succumbed to the 'gaol fever' that was constantly rife and, as the record laconically notes, 'died in prison'.

Agnes Herd is another not learn to from her narrow escape. Having failed to find anyone to speak up for her at her ecclesiastical trial she was excommunicated. But even this did not persuade her to turn over a new leaf, for her name crops up again ten years later in the court roll of the Archdeaconry of Colchester, with the marginal note that she was 'a witch, long-suspected' who was to remain excommunicated while awaiting further process of law.

Darcy's feelings at the outcome of the trials can only be guessed at. Had the accused faced a Continental court they would all without doubt have been burned and he seems to have taken the overall leniency of the verdicts as a personal affront. Soon after the trial ended a pamphlet appeared with the title, *A true and just Recorde, of the Information, Examination and Confession of all the Witches, taken at S. Oses in the countie of Essex: whereof some were executed, and other some entreated according to the determination of lawe.*

The title page also declared that therein 'all men may see what a pestilent people witches are, and how unworthy to live in a Christian Commonwealth.' The Dedication to Thomas, Baron Darcy of Chiche, elaborates

¶A true and iust Recorde, of
the Information, Examination
and Confession of all the Witches, taken at
S. Oses in the countie of Essex: whereof
some were executed, and other some entreated according to the determination of lawe.

Wherein all men may see what a pestilent
people Witches are, and how vnworthy to lyue
in a Christian Common
wealth.

Written orderly, as the ca-
ses were tryed by euidence,
By W. W.

¶*Imprinted in London at the*
three Cranes in the Vinetree by
Thomas Dawson
1582.

on this, asserting that all sorcerers, wizards, witches and wisewomen should be rigorously punished. 'Rigorously said I? Why, it is too mild and gentle a term: I should rather have said most cruelly executed, for that no punishment can be thought upon, be it never so high a degree of torment, which may be deemed sufficient for such a devilish and damnable practice.'

The author is given simply as 'W.W,' but this was almost certainly a cover for Darcy himself. The one-to-one sessions that he conducted in his garden are described in detail, and much of the testimony is stated to have been taken 'by me, Brian Darcy, Esquire.' On several occasions the mask slips even further. Before Elizabeth Bennet makes her confession we are told that 'I, Brian Darcy, directed my warrant for her apprehension.' And after Alice Manfield has made her allegations, 'I, the said Brian, in the presence of the constables and other townspeople of Thorpe, said as 1 had several times before unto her, what a danger it was and how highly she should offend God if she should charge any person with anything untrue.'

Perhaps the clearest evidence of all though is the way that the work is so blatantly designed to display Darcy's witch-hunting zeal and his skill as interrogator and prosecutor. Whatever the verdicts of the court, in the unceasing battle with the Prince of Darkness he was and would remain the people's champion.

SS Peter and Paul, St Osyth

CHAPTER NINE

Despite all Darcy's efforts, witchcraft was far from eliminated from St Osyth. Just two years after the Chelmsford trials three other women, in addition to Margery Barnes/Sammon and her companion, found themselves accused of being witches. Two are named as Alice Bolton and Elizabeth Lomley, while the third, who is simply referred to as Cook's wife, suffered the same fate as Joan Dale and died in prison.

Sporadic cases continued to come before the authorities until in 1645 at least five more local women were caught up in Matthew Hopkins's purge and made the familiar journey to Colchester Gaol.

There is little outward sign in St Osyth today of these far-off events. The surrounding marshland has been largely reclaimed and much of it is now covered by holiday homes and caravan sites, with their attendant takeaways and bingo halls. However, some physical reminders have survived. The cells in the bowels of Colchester Castle can be visited, although the accompanying sound and light display tells the story, not of the St Osyth witch-hunt, but of Hopkins and his hapless victims. The lock-up in St Osyth still stands in Colchester Road, but the tiny building has now been incorporated into a dining room and kitchen extension of the adjoining house, with a bedroom added above the former single-storey structure, although a plaque commemorates Ursula Kemp's five-night sojourn there. Planning permission for this was granted in 1980, despite the Parish Council's preference to convert the building, with its tragic history, into a bus shelter.

The magnificent great hall of St Clere's Hall is now a dining room. The gatehouse through which Darcy's prisoners passed is no more, but the moat continues to encircle most of the house. St Mary's church in Little Oakley, where Richard Harrison preached and prayed, is a private residence, but the surrounding churchyard, complete with gravestones, remains.

The side chapel in St Osyth's church of St Peter and St Paul is traditionally linked with St Clere's Hall. On its south wall an elegant memorial, surmounted by the Darcy arms and crest, declares that 'In this Chapel lieth buried Briant Darcie, Esq, late Highe Sheriffe of ye Countie of Essex ye third son of Thomas Darcie of Tollshunt Darcie in ye said countie' together with his wife Bridget and four of their children two sons and two daughters. The plaque was probably placed there by Darcy's oldest son John, for the dates of his death are left blank and he has his own, far more elaborate alabaster and marble tomb, recording his death in 1638, at the age of seventy-one, on the adjoining wall. Brian Darcy died, fittingly perhaps given his zeal in hunting down the forces of anti-Christ, on Christmas Day, 1587. Although no specific reference is made to his witch-hunting activities, the inscription ends with the pious affirmation: 'Blessed are they that die in ye Lord for they rest from their labour.'

Apart from these survivals in brick and stone, the events that for a fleeting time dominated life in this rural backwater are remembered in other, less tangible ways.

The memorial to Brian Darcy in St Os_ h church

Whatever Darcy hoped to achieve through the publication of the W.W. pamphlet, he can hardly have foreseen the impact it would make. The Essex clergyman George Gifford's *A Dialogue Concerning Witches and Witchcraftes* appeared the following year and satirizes much of the evidence that was so solemnly presented. Samuel, the simple rustic, declares that 'they say there is scarce any town or village in all this shire, but there is one or two witches at the least in it.'

He also echoes the ready acceptance of the existence of familiar spirits that was such a prominent feature of the St Osyth proceedings, 'In good sooth, I may tell it to you as to my friend, when I go into my fields I am afraid, for I see now and then a hare, which my conscience giveth me is a witch or some witch's spirit, she stareth so upon me. And sometimes I see an ugly weasel run through my yard, and there is a foul great cat sometimes in my barn, which I have no liking to.'

Samuel also tells how, at a witch's trial, a man living in a traditional 'longhouse', where human beings and animals lived under the same roof, testified that at one time he had a dun cow that was tied up in the house because it was winter-time. After quarrelling with the accused woman he 'feared that some evil would follow, and for his life he could not come in where the cow was but he must needs take up her tail and kiss under it. Two or three others said that she was by common fame accounted a witch. We found her guilty and she was condemned to prison and to the pillory, but she stood stiff in it that she was no witch.'

The worldly-wise scholar Daniel asks, 'And are you sure she was one?' and when Samuel reminds him of the man 'who could not choose but kiss under his cow's tail' he retorts, 'I say he was far in love with his cow.'

This humorous debunking of the kind of evidence that Darcy so readily accepted was just a prelude to the profound anger that pervades Reginald Scot's *The Discoverie of Witchcraft*. Published in 1584, this is in many ways the most authoritative work on the subject from the entire Elizabethan era, and much of it was inspired directly by W.W.'s account of the events in St Osyth. After several sarcastic asides levelled against Darcy, Scot launches into a full-scale assault on the man and his methods:

> Now, how Brian Darcy's he spirits and she spirits, Titty and Tiffin, Suckin and Pidgin, Liard and Robin etcetra; his white spirits and black spirits, grey spirits and red spirits; devil toad and devil lamb, devil's cat and devil's dam, agree herewithal or can stand consonant with the word of God or true philosophy, let heaven and earth judge. In the meantime, let any man with good consideration peruse that book published by W.W. and it shall suffice to satisfy him in all that may be required touching the vanities of witches' examinations, confessions and executions, where though the tale be told only of the accusers' part without any other answer of theirs than their adversary setteth down ...
>
> And note how and what the witches confess, and see of what weight and importance the causes are;

78

whether their confessions be not won through hope of favour and extorted by flattery or threats, without proof. But insomuch as there were not past seventeen or eighteen condemned at once at St Osyth in the county of Essex, being a whole parish (though of no great quantity) I will say the less, trusting that by this time there remain not many in that parish. If any yet remain, I doubt not but Brian Darcy will find them out. But with what impudency and dishonesty he hath finished it, with what lies and forgeries he hath finished it, what folly and frenzy he hath uttered in it, I am ashamed to report. And therefore, being but a two penny book, I had rather you to buy it and so to peruse it than to fill my book with such beastly stuff.

The literary repercussions do not stop there. Shakespeare's plays contain numerous parallels with the events recorded in the pamphlet. Just as Mary Death's urine was taken to a wiseman, so in *Twelfth Night* Feste ironically offers to carry the 'mad' Malvolio's water to the wisewoman. In *The Tempest* Caliban's mother is a 'damned witch', and Prospero, as a magus, is a superior wiseman practising 'white' magic. Like his humble counterpart Ursula Kemp, he is tempted to cross the narrow line into the black arts and only just in time renounces his 'rough magic'.

Shakespeare's most extensive treatment of witchcraft is of course in *Macbeth*, first produced in 1605 or 1606, following James I's accession to the throne. The Weird Sisters have familiar spirits, Graymalkin, a cat, and Paddock, a toad, and the First Witch creates a storm -

reminiscent of the one that the North Berwick witches supposedly conjured up, almost drowning James and his bride - to gain revenge on the sailor's wife who had refused to give her any of the 'chestnuts in her lap.'

In all of these instances Shakespeare was drawing on the general witchcraft and magic lore of the time, but in the cauldron scene in Act Four, where the Weird Sisters conduct their devilish rituals and make the fatal prophecies to Macbeth, there is a direct link with the St Osyth episode. They create their spell in the presence of Hecate, Queen of the Witches, and their rites end with the stage direction 'Music and a song: Black spirits, etc'. This song appears in full in another play from the period, Thomas Middleton's *The Witch*. For his supernatural elements, Middleton relies heavily on Scot's *Discoverie*, with, for example, Hecate summoning her familiar spirits with the words: 'Titty and Tiffin, Suckin and Pidgen, Liard and Robin! White spirits, black spirits, grey spirits, red spirits! Devil-toad, devil-rat, devil-cat and devil-dam!' There then follows a song, uncannily reminiscent of Thomas Rabbet's damning testimony and Ursula Kemp's and Elizabeth Bennet's fatal confessions, which begins:

> Black spirits and white,
> Red spirits and grey,
> Mingle, mingle, mingle,
> You that mingle may.
>
> Titty, Tiffin keep it stiff in;
> Firedrake, Puckey, make it lucky;
> Liar, Robin, you must bob in.

Simon Forman, a physician with an interest in the occult and an avid theatre-goer, wrote an eye-witness account of a 1611 performance of *Macbeth* at the Globe Theatre. However, he makes no mention of the cauldron scene - one of the most striking episodes in the entire play - and it is likely that it was added for a subsequent revival of the work, to take advantage of the Jacobean theatre-goers' growing appetite for sensationalism.

It is probable therefore that the Hecate sequence was lifted from Middleton's play - there was no such thing as copyright at this time and dramatists and performers were constantly 'borrowing' from one another - and that Shakespeare had no direct hand in it. The feeble doggerel is more likely to arouse laughter than fear today and the episode is omitted from most modern productions.

Even so, it is there in the First Folio text of the plays and has been included in all subsequent editions, and its presence gives a universal immortality to the ephemeral figures who eked out their pathetic existences in an obscure corner of England more than four hundred years ago.

POSTSCRIPT

'Excuse me, sir, but there's a gentleman at the front desk who wants to know if you're interested in buying a witch.'

Cecil Williamson, occultist, demonologist, one time 'Witch Protector to the Royal House of Windsor' and now proprietor of the Museum of Witchcraft, Boscastle, on the north Cornish coast, *was* interested - especially when he learned that what was on offer was the skeleton of a witch put to death nearly four hundred years before. In fact, he was sufficiently intrigued by this 'pig in a poke', as he put it, to agree, after some haggling, on a price of one hundred pounds, and in November, 1963, with his museum closed for the season, he went to St Osyth to collect his purchase. And so it was that life as a public spectacle began once more for Ursula Kemp.

In April, 1582, the two women, Ursula Kemp and Elizabeth Bennet, having been condemned to death, were taken from the Chelmsford courtroom and, without further ado, hanged. Their bodies were then dipped in pitch and left on display - as a dreadful warning of the dangers of dabbling in the occult - for four weeks. They were then, as was the custom returned to their home village but here, at least according to local tradition, they were refused Christian burial and were therefore laid in unconsecrated ground, where they remained undisturbed, their final resting place forgotten, until 1921 when Charles Brooker, a local builder, bought a group of rundown cottages in Mill Street and set about renovating them. He and his family had rented a house in nearby

Colchester Road, not far from the old lock-up where Darcy's victims had been confined, and his daughter Beatrice, who was thirteen years old at the time, vividly recalls her father coming home one day and announcing that, whilst digging for sand in the back garden, he had come across a cluster of bones - human bones. There were two skeletons, lying side by side, and what he thought he had stumbled across was evidence of a double murder.

However, it so happened that two archæologists were working at the time in the nearby Priory and they soon established that the remains, which were both female, were several hundred years old. They had been buried on a north-south axis, instead of the customary east-west, and, most striking of all, before burial iron rivets had been driven through their ankles, knees and wrists. Beatrice was one of the first to view the skeletons and she recalls how the arms were held close to the bodies, with the hands pinned tightly to the thigh bones.

It was clear therefore that what had been uncovered were the remains of two witches, given a non-Christian burial - though within sight of the parish church. They were held down with iron, the traditional metal for combating a witch's powers, to prevent them rising from the dead and bringing renewed terror to the village. And given the dating of the remains, the most likely identities of these two unfortunate creatures are Ursula Kemp and Elizabeth Bennet.

One of the skeletons had been badly damaged in the initial excavation but the other was in a near-complete state. It was of a woman aged between forty-five and fifty, five feet nine inches high - exceptionally tall for a female in Elizabethan times. The thigh bones were unusually long, she was deformed in the left arm and both legs between her knees and ankles, and there was a marked curvature of the spine. The left shoulder was also higher than the right, perhaps as a result of her permanently bowed back.

She will then have been of a striking, not to say, forbidding appearance - similar perhaps to that of Joan Flower in the 1619 woodcut - and this alone will have marked her out as a witch.

The curved back in particular - probably brought about by what we would recognise today as osteoporosis - was enough to achieve this. The witch Sycorax in *The Tempest* was, through age and envy, 'grown into a hoop', and in the Jacobean play *The Witch of Edmonton* by Dekker, Ford and Rowley, based on a real-life case, Mother Sawyer describes herself as 'poor, deform'd, and ignorant and like a bow buckl'd and bent together.'

Ten years before her execution, Ursula Kemp made that fatal visit to the wisewoman at Weeley because of 'lameness in the bones'. The sage which was prescribed for this was also thought to help women 'not only to conceive, but also to retain the birth without miscarrying' - and just a year or so later her son Thomas was born. So it is at least possible that these were her remains, lying within yards of the spot where she had met Grace Thurlow and been told that, thanks to her efforts, young Davey had been cured.

Charles Brooker was allowed to keep his discovery and, being of an enterprising turn of mind, he constructed a wooden frame around the better preserved skeleton, put a double trap-door on top and surrounded it with iron railings. He then allowed access to the curious, on payment of an appropriate fee, had postcards and souvenir leaflets printed, and before long regular charabanc outings were being run from Clacton-on-Sea to view 'the St Osyth skeleton.'

One visitor, who was taken by her father, recalls how the group was conducted 'with all due ceremony to the graveside' and there regaled with the hair-raising tale of how the unlucky woman had been placed in a ducking stool and immersed three times in the village mill pool. When her drowned body rose to the surface, a sure sign that she was indeed a witch, she was shackled with the iron rivets - still there, impaled in her thighs and knees - and buried at that very spot.

But then, in the winter of 1933, disaster struck. Charles Brooker and his family - there were three girls and a boy - were living in the Mill Street cottage, by now known locally as the 'Skeleton House'. The living room fire was still burning when they went to bed and during the night the oak chimney beam smouldered then caught alight. Luckily, the boy was sleeping downstairs and the family, still in their night-clothes, escaped before the roof came crashing down. One of the daughters, Constance, was sleeping next door, keeping company with a friend who suffered nightmares - hardly surprising, perhaps, with what lay in the neighbouring garden, although Constance herself had no such terrors. 'I had a very happy childhood there,' she says, 'and I was certainly not afraid of any curse.'

Even so, she too had to flee for her life, while another neighbour, Mrs Curtis, eighty-five years old and an invalid, had to be carried from her bed by three men with her bedroom already ablaze. In all, four of the timbered cottages were badly damaged but the fire brigade, drawing water from the mill-pond a quarter of a mile away, saved the remaining houses in the street. However - at least according to local legend - in the darkness and confusion one of the firemen put his foot through the trapdoors over the skeleton and broke his hip. Whatever the truth of this, the fire was soon put down to supernatural forces, with the witches wreaking vengeance on those who had disturbed them.

The skeleton itself was roughly covered in orange linoleum taken from the ruined kitchen floor, the grave was filled in with earth and debris and remained untouched until 1957 when John Scolding, husband of Constance and as enterprising as his father-in-law, attempted to reinstate the witch's sideshow. The idea was not well received in the village though and planning permission for an adjacent car park was refused. But then, six years later, with a developer expressing interest in the site - a five-bedroom, two garage modern house stands there today - he made the journey to Boscastle.

When, on a frosty November morning, Cecil Williamson arrived in St Osyth to his surprise he was met by a gaggle of journalists and a news crew from Anglia

Television. Fortified by cups of tea from nearby residents and with the cameras turning, he dug his way into the cavity. Five feet down he reached the linoleum and when, with shaking hands, he drew this aside, the bones were revealed.

After assembling them on half a dozen baker's fancy-cake trays, he was delighted to find that the skeleton was complete and apparently unharmed. Two of the wicked-looking rivets - almost a foot long - had also survived, and the remnants of a third were still embedded in the right thigh bone. So he carefully packed everything on a bedding of upholsterer's cotton wool and returned to Cornwall with his booty.

Unequivocally identified as the 'mortal remains of Ursula Kemp' and lying in a specially constructed open elm coffin, lined with satin of royal purple, it became the prize exhibit in his museum. Over the years, many St Osyth people, including Charles Brooker's daughter Beatrice, visited the display, either out of curiosity or to pay their respects to their former fellow resident. In the 1980's it moved with him to Buckfast in Devon, to the House of Shells. Cecil Williamson's wife had built up a large collection of sea shells from many lands, but it is also worth noting that he had an impish sense of humour and one of his previous establishments had been called the House of Spells - and that the Buckfast residence is now run as a retreat house by the monks of the nearby Abbey.

In February 1982, on the four hundredth anniversary of the case, the BBC broadcast a dramatised radio documentary, *Witch-hunt in St Osyth*. The programme created a renewed flurry of interest in the story and there was even some debate as to whether Ursula Kemp should be returned to her original home. The Parish Council therefore approached her current owner, asking 'under what conditions you would release the remains of Ursula Kemp, if at all.'

But Cecil Williamson's response was typically cryptic, with the advice that they should 'let sleeping dogs lie.' The Council would only he bringing trouble on themselves, he declared, if they brought the remains back to the village. His museum had aroused controversy on numerous occasions, with various Christian bodies in particular attempting to close it down.

At Bourton-on-the-Water in the Cotswolds, where it had previously been set up, he had been denounced from the pulpit of the parish church - and, according to Williamson's own account, his cause had not been helped by his priestly assailant dropping dead three weeks later from a heart attack.

He was, in any case, reluctant to part with the remains, for over the years he had built up quite a rapport with them. 'I would,' he said, 'never dream of going into the museum without having a chat to her.' And to a correspondent he wrote: 'Lucky old Ursula. Done to death in 1582, yet in 1982 she lies snug and warm, and well cared for with a deal of affection from those who see and come to know her. Maybe there is a touch of magic somewhere in all this.'

However, by 1998, and in his ninetieth year, he was

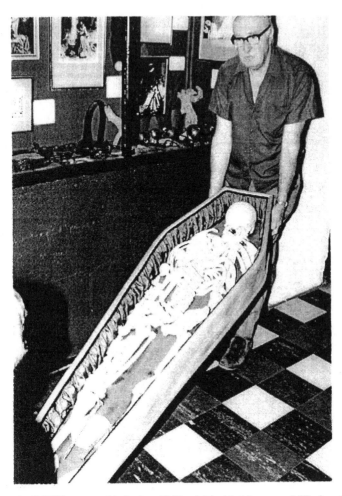

Cecil Williamson with 'lucky old Ursula' in his Museum of Witchcraft at Boscastle

conscious that he would not be able to care for her for very much longer. He considered having her 'mortal remains' disposed of along with his own but finally, just months before his death in December 1999, the skeleton passed into new hands. Still lying in its half-coffin and on its bed of satin, it remains in the south-west of England, housed temporarily in a former church - in what was at one time, because of the locality's dissolute reputation, known as Damnation Alley - whilst a more permanent home is established.

It will then take its place alongside other artifacts relating to witchcraft and magic practices from the mid-fifteenth century onwards, and will complement the specialist library of over two hundred thousand volumes - many of them extremely rare, in some cases unique - concerned with obsessive and fanatical beliefs.

The bones are in a very fragile state, many of them in a much worse condition than is indicated by the photographs from the 1920's. The upper set of teeth, which was near complete, has all but gone, and Williamson, in his reconstruction fitted the right femur back to front into what remains of the matching pelvis. Both femurs are now fractured in several places and this is particularly unfortunate because in the early photographs one appears to be larger than the other - a pointer to what could be a final twist in the story.

One clear anomaly is still apparent: there are three hip joints - one being placed below the right shoulder blade - whereas, as Dickens put it of Mr Squeers's one eye, the popular prejudice runs to two. This would seem to confirm the suspicion that at some time - probably before it was first put on show - one complete (or rather over-complete) skeleton was assembled from the two sets of remains. If this is the case, it is likely that what has been preserved is an amalgam of both Ursula Kemp and Elizabeth Bennet - and as they suffered, died and were buried side by side, surely this is only fitting.

The room where the remains currently rest is dedicated to Philosophy, with a portrait of the seventeenth century philosopher John Locke looking down on the scene. It is surely a fine irony that today, alongside students preparing their doctoral theses in what was formerly the church of Christ the Saviour, lie these two simple, illiterate women, who for their sins - real or imagined - were refused Christian burial over four centuries ago.

Charabanc trips to view the 'St Osyth skeleton' were run from the surrounding area

FURTHER READING

At least three copies of the 1582 pamphlet *A true and just Recorde...* have survived and are located in the British Library and the libraries of Corpus Christi College, Oxford, and Trinity College, Cambridge. A facsimile edition, with an introduction by Anthony Harris, was published in 1981 by Scholars' Facsimiles and Reprints, Delmar, New York, USA.

An edition of Reginald Scot's *The Discoverie of Witchcraft* (1584), edited by Brinsley Nicholson, was published in 1886 and reprinted in 1973.

George Gifford's *A Dialogue Concerning Witches and Witchcraftes* (1583) was reprinted in Shakespeare Association Facsimiles No 1 (1931).

The Witch can be found in *The Works of Thomas Middleton Vol. 5*, edited by A H Bullen (Mermaid Edition, 1885-6).

For a detailed, comprehensive study of witchcraft in Essex in the sixteenth and seventeenth centuries see *Witchcraft in Tudor and Stuart England, a regional study* (1970) by A D J Macfarlane.

Other relevant works include:

Witch Hunting and Witch Trials (1929), C H L'Estrange Ewen; *Calendar of Assize Records: Essex Indictments, Elizabeth I* (1978), ed. J S Cockburn; *The History and Antiquities of the County of Essex* (1763-8, reprinted 1978), Philip Morant; *The St Osyth Witch Story, 1582 and all that* (1993), compiled by Phyl Hendy; *Broomstick over Essex and East Anglia* (1981), by Tom Gardiner.

INDEX